I0164990

Time with Our Holy Mother

A Prayer Diary
Devoted to
The Virgin Mary

ISBN: 978-0692936528

DEDICATED,
WITH MUCH LOVE,
TO MY MOM
JUDITH WARD BOYER

My Prayer Diary

Name: _____

If you ever feel distressed during your day,
call upon our Lady, just say this simple prayer:
"Mary, Mother of Jesus, please be a mother to me now."
I must admit, this prayer has never failed me.

- Blessed Mother Teresa

Mary's Song of Praise
Luke 1:46-49

My soul magnifies the Lord,
and my spirit rejoices
in God my Savior,
for He has regarded the
low estate of His handmaiden.
For behold, henceforth
all generations will call me blessed;
for He who is mighty
has done great things for me,
and holy is His name.

Hail, holy Queen, mother of mercy,
our life, our sweetness and our hope.
To thee do we cry, poor banished
children of Eve. To thee do we send up
our sighs, mourning and weeping in
this valley of tears. Turn then, most
gracious advocate, thine eyes of mercy
toward us, and after this our exile,
show unto us the blessed fruit of thy
womb, Jesus. O clement, O loving, O
sweet Virgin Mary! Pray for us, O holy
Mother of God, that we may be made
worthy of the promises of Christ.
Amen

- Liturgy of the Hours

Remember, O most gracious Virgin Mary, that never was it known that any one who fled to thy protection, implored thy help or sought thy intercession, was left unaided. Inspired by this confidence, I fly unto thee, O Virgin of virgins my Mother; to thee do I come, before thee I stand, sinful and sorrowful; O Mother of the Word Incarnate, despise not my petitions, but in thy mercy hear and answer me, Amen

- Saint Bernard of Clairvaux

Loving Mother of the Redeemer,
Gate of heaven, star of the sea,
Assist your people of have fallen
yet strive to rise again. To the
wonderment of nature you bore
your Creator, yet remained a
virgin after as before. You who
received Gabriel's joyful greeting,
have pity on us poor sinners.
Amen.

- Hermann the Lame

Even while living in the world, the heart of Mary was so filled with motherly tenderness and compassion for men that no-one ever suffered so much for their own pains, as Mary suffered for the pains of her children.

- *Saint Jerome*

As mariners are guided into port
by the shining of a star,
so Christians are guided
to heaven by Mary.

- Saint Thomas Aquinas

Let us entrust to her intercession the daily prayer for peace, especially in places where the senseless logic of violence is most ferocious; so that all people may be convinced that in this world we must help each other, as brothers and sisters, to build the civilization of love.

- Pope Benedict XVI

Jesus cannot be understood without his Mother.

– Pope Francis

Some people are so foolish
that they think they can go
through life without the help
of the Blessed Mother.

- Saint Padre Pio

.

From Mary we learn
to surrender to God's
Will in all things.

From Mary we learn
to trust even when all
hope seems gone.

From Mary we learn
to love Christ her Son
and the Son of God!

- Saint John Paul II

Never be afraid of loving the Blessed Virgin too much. You can never love her more than Jesus did.

- Saint Maximilian Kolbe

And the angel said
to her, "Do not be
afraid, Mary, for
you have found
favor with God."
    - Luke 1:30

And the angel came to her and said, "Hail, Mary, full of grace, the Lord is with you!"

- Luke 1:28

She is so full of love that no one who asks for her intercession is rejected, no matter how sinful he may be.

- Saint Louis de Montfort

Mary is the lily in God's garden.

- Bridget of Sweden

Such is the will of God that we should have everything through Mary.

- Saint Alphonsus Liguori

Mary's role in the Church is inseparable from her union with Christ and flows directly from it.

- Catechism of the Catholic Church

Let us run to Mary,
and, as her little children,
cast ourselves into her arms
with a perfect confidence.

- *Saint Francis de Sales*

To desire grace without recourse to the Virgin Mother is to desire to fly without wings.

- Pope Pius XII

The reason why Christ is unknown today is because His Mother is unknown.

- Blessed Cardinal John Henry Newman

To give worthy praise to the Lord's mercy, we unite ourselves with your immaculate mother, for then our hymn will be more pleasing to you, because she is chosen from among men and angels. Through her, as through a pure crystal, your mercy was passed on to us. Through her, man became pleasing to God; Through her, streams of grace flowed down upon us.

- *Saint Faustina*

So your strength is failing you? Why don't you tell your mother about it?...Mother! Call her with a loud voice. She is listening to you; she sees you in danger, perhaps, and she--your holy mother Mary--offers you, along with the grace of her son, the refuge of her arms, the tenderness of her embrace...and you will find yourself with added strength for the new battle.

- Saint Josemaria Escriva

No man is delivered or preserved from the world-wide snares of Satan save through Mary; and God grants His graces to no one except through her alone.

- Saint Germanus

If the hurricanes of temptation rise against you, or you are running upon the rocks of trouble, look to the star - call on Mary!

- Saint Bernard of Clairvaux

Believe me, there is no more powerful means to obtain God's grace than to employ the intercessions of the Holy Virgin.

- Saint Philip Neri

Mary is the most sweet bait, chosen, prepared, and ordained by God, to catch the hearts of men.

- Saint Catherine of Siena

Mary is the sure path to our meeting with Christ. Devotion to the Mother of the Lord, when it is genuine, is always an impetus to a life guided by the spirit and values of the Gospel.

- Saint John Paul II

In trial or difficulty I have recourse
to Mother Mary, whose glance alone
is enough to dissipate every fear.

- *Saint Therese of Lisieux*

And when Elizabeth heard the greeting of Mary, the babe leaped in her womb; and Elizabeth was filled with the Holy Spirit and she exclaimed with a loud cry, "Blessed are you among women, and blessed is the fruit of your womb! And why is this granted me, that the mother of my Lord should come to me?"

- Luke 1:41-45

.

Men do not fear a powerful hostile army as the powers of hell fear the name and protection of Mary.

- Saint Bonaventure

www.ingramcontent.com/pod-product-compliance
Lightning Source LLC
Chambersburg PA
CBHW070543030426
42337CB00016B/2322